KU-508-625

The best 100 tapas

EDICIONES
Aldeasa

Introduction

It used to be common practice in Spain for people to call into a bar or two just before lunch for a *chato de vino tinto* (glass of red wine).

The first very simple *tapas* – snacks or appetisers – arose from the need to avoid drinking on an empty stomach and consisted of slices of bread topped with raw ingredients and combined with cold meat, cheese, tinned fish and mayonnaise or oil. As the country developed, people began to work longer hours and have less time for leisure pursuits and calling into bars. *Tapas* began to replace full lunches a number of years ago and have now become commonplace. Factors such as the quality and diversity of Spanish cuisine have also ensured that *tapas* have become the norm rather than the exception. Depending on the region or place, *tapas* may also be referred to as *pinchos* or *banderillas*. The change of name does not however affect the product, which is always served in small portions. In addition to the *tapas* served on bread, individual dishes of typical Spanish stews have now also become popular. Unless otherwise indicated, recipes are calculated for six servings. Finally, thanks to Soni Herreros de Tejada for her collaboration in this book, which aims to serve only as an introduction to the art of *tapas*, since not even an encyclopaedia would be large enough to describe the infinite number of combinations that exist and that are nothing short of the quest for a harmony of flavours, in much the same way as a musician searches for the notes to create a melody.

vegetables and mushrooms

Ajo blanco con uvas
Cold garlic soup with grapes

- 250 g breadcrumbs
- 150 g raw almonds, crushed
- 1 clove of garlic, without shoots
- 1 egg
- 2 tablespoons vinegar

- 1 glass olive oil, maximum acidity 0.4°
- 1/2 litre water

GARNISH:
- 100 g grapes
- 50 g currants and salt

let's get started

Soak the breadcrumbs for one hour and then strain. • Crush all the ingredients in a blender for 5 minutes and then in a food mill. • Place the mixture in a refrigerator to cool. If the mixture is too thick, add ice or more water.

Presentation: Garnish with grapes and currants.

Barquitas rellenas de espárragos
Asparagus pastries

- **Dough for pastries (see recipe, p.117)**
- **12 asparagus**

- **Mayonnaise sauce (see recipe, p.116)**

---

let's get started

Pastries: Prepare using the same procedure as in the recipe, but with half the ingredients.
• Once prepared, place the dough in a pastry bag with a nozzle 1/2 cm in diameter. • Make sticks measuring around 6 centimetres and place on a tray lined with greaseproof paper. • Bake in the oven at 180° for 20 minutes. • Stuffing: Cut off the tips of the asparagus to match the size of the boats. • Prepare your own mayonnaise or buy ready-made.
Presentation: Slice open the boats with a sharp knife and stuff with mayonnaise and asparagus.

Berenjenas con queso

Aubergines with cheese

- 2 medium-sized aubergines
- 1 Camembert cheese
- 6 tablespoons tomato sauce (p. 115)

- Oregano, chopped
- Special flour for batter
- 2 dl olive oil

let's get started

Peel the aubergines and cut lengthwise into strips 1/2 cm wide. • Place in a bowl of salted water for 10 minutes. • Strain well and roll in flour, then fry in very hot oil until crunchy.

Presentation: Coat the aubergines in tomato sauce and cover with large pieces of Camembert cheese. • Sprinkle with oregano and serve.

Crêpes rellenas de setas con besamel

Pancakes stuffed with wild mushrooms and béchamel sauce

- 12 pancakes, readymade or homemade (see recipe, p. 117)
- 500 g wild mushrooms
- 1 spring onion, chopped
- 2 garlic cloves, chopped
- 3 tablespoons oil
- 10 tablespoons béchamel sauce (see recipe, p. 114)
- 1 small tin Estivium truffles

let's get started

Pancakes: Prepare the pancakes according to the recipe. • **Stuffing:** Prepare the béchamel sauce then cover with cling film and leave to cool. • Sauté the onion in a deep frying pan until transparent then add the garlic. • Remove any earth from the wild mushrooms, then remove the stalks and add to the sauté. • Cook together until any resulting liquid evaporates. • Season and mix with the béchamel sauce.

Presentation: Distribute the stuffing among the pancakes, then fold each pancake in four to form a triangle. • Sprinkle with chopped Estivium truffles.

Champiñones rellenos con gambas y jamón
Mushrooms stuffed with prawns and ham

- 6 mushrooms
- 6 king prawn tails
- 50 g shavings Iberian ham

- 3 garlic cloves, chopped
- 1 1/2 dl olive oil
- Chopped parsley

let's get started

Stuffing: Peel the king prawns tails and fry in a little oil. Set aside. • **Mushrooms:** Select the largest mushrooms for stuffing and hollow the inside of the cap. • Fry the chopped garlic, sprinkle with parsley and stuff the mushrooms with the mixture. • Pour over any remaining fat. • Place in an oven pre-heated to 160° for 20 minutes.

Presentation: Remove the mushrooms from oven and add the ham shavings and fried king prawns.

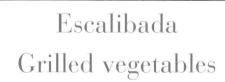

Escalibada
Grilled vegetables

- **2 potatoes**
- **2 onions**
- **2 green peppers**

- **2 aubergines**
- **Salt**
- **Virgin olive oil**

let's get started

Wash the vegetables and potatoes, chop them into very thin rings and arrange in a large ovenproof dish. • Sprinkle with salt then finger sprinkle a little oil over the top. • Cover with tinfoil and roast for 30 minutes at 170º. • Remove from the oven. • Then cook au gratin under an oven grill when this is very hot. Remove when the vegetables begin to toast. Drizzle again with virgin olive oil.

Note: This dish is of Catalan origin. Traditionally the vegetables were charcoal-grilled in different batches depending on the cooking requirements. Here the recipe has been simplified.

Gazpacho

- 250 g bread
- 1 kg ripe red tomatoes
- 1 green pepper
- 1 garlic clove
- 50 g cucumber
- 1 dl oil
- 1 tablespoon vinegar
- Salt and a pinch of sugar

- Water and ice

ACCOMPANIMENT:
- 1/2 cucumber
- 1/2 green pepper
- 1 *piquillo* pepper, tinned
- 1/2 onion
- 1 hard-boiled egg
- Fried diced bread

let's get started

Soak the breadcrumbs for a few hours. • Place the previously strained bread, tomatoes, pepper, cucumber, garlic, oil, salt, sugar and a small glass of water in an electric blender. • Crush for a few minutes to obtain a consistent blend. • Put it through a food mill then pour into a bowl. If the soup is very thick, add a little water to thin it down.

Presentation: Serve with ice cubes. Cut the vegetables and egg separately. • Arrange the accompaniment around the gazpacho or on a separate tray.

Habas a la catalana
Catalan-style broad beans

- 1 kg broad beans
- 200 g Catalan sausage
- 2 slices of bacon, chopped
- 2 garlic cloves
- 1 onion, chopped

- 1 small glass *oloroso* sherry
- 1 small glass olive oil
- 8 sprigs mint, chopped
- Salt

let's get started

Shell the beans. We also recommend removing the pod. Set aside. • Lightly fry the chopped onions and garlic cloves in a clay casserole, then add the bacon. Once all the ingredients are transparent, add the beans. • Cover the mixture with water. • Add the sherry, two sprigs of chopped mint, salt and water to cover. • Cook the beans until tender. • Chop the white Catalan sausage into slices and add.

Presentation: Serve in the same clay casserole and garnish with the remaining chopped mint.

Melón con jamón
Melon with ham

- **1 yellow melon**
- **100 g ham**

let's get started

Cut the melon in half and then each half into three slices. • Remove the seeds and cut the slices into pieces measuring approximately 2.5 cm. • Cut the ham into very fine slices, of a size to cover each piece of melon.

Presentation: Wrap the slices of ham around the pieces of melon and place on a metal or wooden skewer.

Paella de verduras
Vegetable paella

- 100 g leek (white part), chopped
- 100 g onion, chopped
- 150 g mushroom, washed and finely sliced
- 1 l water and pinch of salt
- 150 g cabbage, cut into strips

- 150 g peas, frozen
- 150 g green beans, chopped into small squares
- 150 g baby carrots, frozen
- 1 vegetable stock cube
- 3 strands of saffron
- 2 tablespoons tomato sauce (p. 115)

- 475 g (two large cups) Calasparra rice
- 4 large cups of stock and a few drops of lemon
- 1 1/2 dl olive oil, maximum acidity 0.4°
- 1 large sweet red pepper and 1 hard-boiled egg

let's get started

Pour 1/2 dl oil into the paellera (special large frying pan for preparing paella) with leek, onion and mushrooms. Lightly fry until all the liquid evaporates. • Cook the remaining vegetables in a pan then add to the mushroom sauté. • Add the rice and the remaining oil to the paellera and sauté until the rice turns opaque. • Drizzle with lemon juice and season generously. • Add 4 large cups of hot water and when it water begins to boil, place in an oven at 180° for 20 minutes. Taste the rice to check whether it is cooked. If it is still hard, cover for 5 minutes.

Presentation: Serve the rice in the paellera itself or in 6 individual dishes garnished with the sweet red pepper and 1 slice of hard-boiled egg.

Pan con tomate, ajo y perejil
Bread with tomato, garlic and parsley

- French bread (baguette)
- 6 tomatoes
- 6 tablespoons bread crumbs
- 2 garlic cloves
- 6 tablespoons parsley
- 1 tablespoon paprika

- 6 teaspoons olive oil
- Salt, sugar and parsley

TOMATO PURÉE:
- 2 garlic cloves
- 3 tablespoons oil
- Salt
- A pinch of sugar

let's get started

Place the tomatoes on their flattest side. • Cut just above the middle and empty the contents. Set the tomato pulp aside. • Season the tomatoes with salt and a pinch of sugar and turn upside down so that the liquid runs off. • Turn right side up and fill with the finely chopped mixture of garlic, parsley, bread crumbs, paprika and olive oil. • Roast for 20 minutes at 160°.
• **Tomato purée:** Crush the tomato pulp set aside earlier in an electric blender together with the garlic, oil, salt and a pinch of sugar.
Presentation: Cut the bread into 6 small slices and coat with the crushed tomato. Place a roasted tomato on top of each slice. • Sprinkle with parsley and serve.

Patatas a la brava

Spicy potatoes

- 700 g potatoes
- 1/2 l tomato sauce (p. 115)
- 1 small piece of chili pepper or a little Tabasco sauce

- 6 tablespoons olive oil
- Abundant oil for frying

let's get started

Peel the potatoes and chop roughly. • Fry in abundant oil and set aside. Fry the chili pepper in oil and pour over the potatoes. • Add the tomato sauce, covering them well but without saturating.

Presentation: Serve on a plate or in 6 individual dishes.

Patatas al alioli
Alioli potatoes (in garlic and oil sauce)

- **750 g potatoes**
- ***Alioli* (garlic and oil) sauce (see recipe, p. 114)**
- **1 tablespoon mild mustard**

- **1 tablespoon sea salt**
- **Table salt**
- **1 pinch of recently crushed pepper**

let's get started

Peel the potatoes and chop them up into pieces of the size shown in the photograph. • Cook in water with sea salt until tender but not to the point that they break up. • Strain and leave to cool. Mix with the alioli sauce and season to taste.

Presentation: Serve on a plate or in 6 individual dishes.

Picadillo helado cordobés
Iced Cordoba *Picadillo* (diced vegetable salad)

- 2 ripe but firm tomatoes
- 2 cucumbers
- 1 marrow
- 2 green peppers

- 1 spring onion
- Olive oil
- Sherry vinegar
- Salt and a pinch sugar

let's get started

Chop up the cucumbers, tomato, peppers and spring onion. Wash the marrow and dice the skin. Set aside. • **Vinaigrette dressing:** dissolve the salt, sugar and pepper in a teaspoon of sherry vinegar and stir well with the oil.

Presentation: Mix the vegetables with the vinaigrette dressing and serve very cold with two ice cubes on top.

Note: Less ripe cucumbers are easier to digest.

Pimientos del piquillo rellenos de bacalao
Piquillo (roasted red) peppers stuffed with cod

- 200 g salted cod, sliced
- 1 tin *piquillo* peppers (around 425 g); set aside 2 peppers for the sauce

- Béchamel sauce (see recipe, p.114)
- A few drops of meat stock
- Salt

let's get started

Cut the cod into pieces and soak for 48 hours. • Store in a refrigerator and change the water around 6 times. • To prepare, place the cod pieces in cold water and heat but remove before boiling. Skin and bone and then crumble. • Prepare the béchamel sauce and divide into two portions. • Add the cod to one portion, bring to the boil then remove from heat. Use this to stuff the peppers then place in an ovenproof dish. • **Pepper sauce:** Add peppers and meat stock to the other portion of béchamel sauce. • After mixing in an electric blender, pour over the ovenproof dish and oven cook for 1/2 hour at 180°.

Pimientos rellenos de cangrejo y carabinero

Piquillo (red roasted) peppers stuffed with crab and large red shrimp

---

- Baguette-style bread
- 6 *piquillo* peppers, tinned
- 200 g crab meat, tinned
- 2 large red shrimps
- Mayonnaise sauce (see recipe, p. 116)

- Laurel leaves
- 2 tablespoons olive oil
- 1 tablespoon Express cornflour
- Capers

---

let's get started

Boil the large red shrimps in a little salted water with 2 laurel leaves. • Once they have boiled for 2 minutes, remove and leave to cool. Peel and dice. Boil the heads and skins in 3/4 litre of the same water. Strain and put through a food mill. Prepare a sauce by thickening 1/2 litre of this liquid with the cornflour and bring to the boil. Leave to cool then mix with mayonnaise; for this recipe the mayonnaise must be very thick and prepared without vinegar. • Mix in the crab meat with the large red shrimps and sauce. • Stuff the peppers with this mixture.
Presentation: Cut the bread into 6 small slices, place a stuffed pepper on each slice and garnish with capers.

Pimientos rellenos de morcilla
Peppers stuffed with *morcilla* (Spanish black pudding)

- **12** *piquillo* **peppers**
- **2** *morcillas*, **200 g each**
- **1/2 l tomato sauce (p. 115)**

- **3 tablespoons cream**
- **Salt**
- **Pepper**

let's get started

Prepare the tomato sauce and add the cream. • Skin the *morcillas*, chop up the meat and fry, stirring continuously for a few minutes. • Stuff the peppers with the *morcilla*. • Place the peppers on a base of tomato sauce in individual ovenproof dishes, sprinkling with a few drops of oil. • Bake at 170° for 15 minutes. • Serve hot.

Pimientos rojos y ventresca

Red peppers and *ventresca* breast of tuna

- 6 slices of *chapata* (rustic-style bread)
- 3 red peppers (around 200 g)
- 50 g onion

- 100 g *ventresca* tuna in olive oil, tinned
- 5 tablespoons olive oil, maximum acidity 0.4°

let's get started

Cover the peppers with tinfoil and roast for 1 hour. Leave to cool without removing the tinfoil.
• Peel and cut into strips. • In a frying pan, lightly fry the finely chopped onion and peppers in the oil.

Presentation: Serve the fried peppers on 6 slices of bread. • Place strips of Ventresca tuna on top. *Ventresca* is the breast of tuna fish and is extremely juicy and tender.

Note: *Ventresca* is more expensive than tuna, so ordinary tuna can be used instead.

Pisto

Ratatouille

- **500 g marrows, peeled and diced**
- **300 g green peppers, finely chopped**
- **100 g onion, chopped**

- **150 g tomatoes, poached and peeled**
- **1 red pepper**
- **Olive oil**
- **Salt, pepper and sugar**
- **2 hard-boiled eggs, for garnish**

let's get started

Wrap the red pepper in tinfoil and roast for 1 hour. • Cover and leave to cool, then peel and dice. • Sauté the onion in 2 dl oil. After 5 minutes, add the green peppers. 15 minutes later, add the marrows and red pepper. Season and simmer gently. • After 1/2 hour, add the tomatoes and cook everything together over a low heat for another 10 minutes. • Finally, leave to settle and remove any fat floating on the surface. • If there is still too much liquid, leave to cook a little longer and add salt and pepper.
Presentation: Serve in 6 individual dishes garnished with hard-boiled eggs sliced diagonally.

Salmorejo

Cold tomato and garlic soup

- 1 kg ripe tomatoes
- 1 clove of garlic
- 1 large cup bread crumbs
- 1/4 l olive oil
- 1 teaspoon vinegar (optional)

- A pinch of sugar
- Salt
- 100 g Jabugo ham, cut into strips
- 2 hard-boiled eggs, chopped

let's get started

Place the tomatoes and garlic cloves in the electric blender. • Crush, add the bread crumbs and blend a little more. • Gradually add oil while blending. • Once all the oil has been added, season and crush again at maximum speed for 2 minutes to obtain an even blend. • Place in the refrigerator.

Presentation: Serve very cold in individual bowls accompanied by ham shavings and hard-boiled egg.

Tartaletas de champiñones a la crema
Mushroom tartlets à la crème

- 6 tartlets made from frozen or home-made pastry (see recipe, p. 118)
- 1/2 kg mushrooms
- 1/2 onion, finely chopped
- 50 g bacon, finely chopped
- 2 tablespoons instant onion soup
- 1 tablespoon flour

- 1/4 l cream
- 1 teaspoon Worcestershire sauce (Perrins)
- 75 g butter
- 2 tablespoons olive oil
- Salt

let's get started

Remove the caps from the mushrooms and wash under running tap water without submerging. • Cut into slices, set aside and cover to prevent from browning and changing colour. • Fry bacon in butter mixed with oil; when crunchy, add the onion. • After 5 minutes add the mushrooms, cover and simmer gently. • **Sauce:** Poor the cold cream into the flour, stir continuously and bring to the boil. Add the onion soup and Perrins sauce, stirring continuously. • After 5 minutes stir into the mushrooms.
Presentation: Distribute the mixture between 6 tartlets.

Tartaletas de ensaladilla rusa

Russian salad tartlets

- 6 readymade or homemade pastry tartlets (see recipe, p. 118)
- 200 g potatoes, peeled and diced
- 250 g peas, podded
- 250 g beetroot (optional)
- 250 g carrots, washed and diced
- 1/4 l mayonnaise sauce, readymade or homemade (see recipe, p.116)
- Salt and pepper

let's get started

Cook the carrots and peas together. After 15 minutes add the potatoes and salt. • Leave to cool then stir in mayonnaise slowly to avoid saturating vegetables with the sauce.

Presentation: Distribute the mixture between 6 tartlets.

Note: If you use beetroot, cook in a pressure cooker for 20 minutes without removing the skin or shoots. • Once cold, peel and dice. Beetroot can also be purchased tinned or jarred.

eggs

Crêpes rellenas de revuelto de pimientos

Pancakes stuffed with scrambled eggs and *piquillo* (roasted red) peppers

---

- 12 pancakes, frozen or homemade (see recipe, p. 117)
- 6 *piquillo* peppers, tinned
- 1 onion, chopped

- 4 eggs
- 2 hard-boiled eggs, for garnish
- 3 tablespoons olive oil
- Salt

---

let's get started

If you buy the pancakes frozen, thaw at room temperature. Set aside. • Chop up the peppers and fry lightly for around 15 minutes. • Whisk the eggs and mix with the peppers and any fat that they may have released in the frying pan. • Stir over a moderate heat until the egg sets. • Remove the frying pan from the heat and continue to stir. The eggs should remain fluffy.
Presentation: Distribute the stuffing among the pancakes and fold each pancake into four to form a triangle. • Sprinkle with the chopped hard-boiled eggs.

Huevos duros rellenos rebozados
Stuffed hard-boiled eggs in batter

- 6 eggs
- 100 g chorizo sausage
- Béchamel sauce (p. 114) with 50 g flour
- 2 hard-boiled eggs
- Flour
- Bread crumbs
- Abundant olive oil for frying

let's get started

Prepare the béchamel sauce with 50 g flour and the same amount of ingredients as indicated in the recipe. • Remove the skin of the chorizo sausage, chop up finely and add to the béchamel sauce. Cook for 1 minute. • Cook the eggs in salted water for 15 minutes, then cool under running tap water and shell. • Cut the eggs in half, remove the yolks and chop up finely.
• Stuffing: Mix the egg yolks with the chorizo sausage béchamel sauce. • Use this to stuff the white of the eggs, creating a domed shape. • Roll in flour and beaten egg and fry in abundant hot oil.

Huevos estrellados sobre patatas
Potatoes with fried eggs

- 1 1/2 kg potatoes
- 2 garlic cloves, peeled
- 6 medium-sized eggs
- Salt
- Abundant olive oil

let's get started

Peel the potatoes and cut into strips, approximately 3/4 centimetres thick. When the oil reaches a temperature of 175°, fry the potatoes in several batches. Control the heat so that the potatoes cook inside without browning. Once cooked, place them in a colander. • Leave a film of oil in the frying pan and add the potatoes once again. • Whilst re-heating, break the eggs intentionally one by one over the potatoes. • Season to taste.

Huevos rellenos de atún

Eggs stuffed with tuna

- 6 eggs
- 2 *piquillo* peppers
- Mayonnaise, readymade or homemade (see recipe, p. 116)

- 2 tablespoons oil
- 1 tin tuna in olive oil
- French bread (baguette)

let's get started

Boil the eggs in cold water with salt for 15 minutes. Remove the shells under cold running water to stop them from cooking. Chop them in half and remove the yolks. To enable them to stand upright, cut a small slice off the domed area. • Stuffing: Crush the chopped yolk and chopped pepper, the crumbled tuna and 2 or 3 tablespoons of mayonnaise.

Presentation: Stuff the egg whites and place them on 6 slices of bread. • Chop up 1 pepper into 6 small squares and garnish each egg.

Revuelto de ajetes
Srambled eggs with spring garlic

- 100 g tender spring garlic
- 4 eggs
- 2 tablespoons cream
- Salt

- 3 tablespoons oil
- 6 tartlet cases made from readymade or homemade pastry (see recipe, p. 118)

let's get started

Cut the spring garlic stems in half and chop into strips measuring approximately 3 cm, using only the white portions. • Fry lightly in a frying pan with oil until soft, then season accordingly. • Beat the eggs, add a pinch of salt and mix in the cream. • Pour the mixture into the frying pan with the spring garlic. • Stir until the eggs set and the mixture acquires a creamy consistency. **Presentation:** Serve in the tartlet cases.

Tortilla de calabacín
Marrow omelette

- 6 eggs
- 2 dl oil
- Readymade mayonnaise
- 1 kg marrows, unpeeled

- 2 onions, finely cut
- Salt
- *Chapata* (rustic-style bread)

let's get started

Fry the onions slowly in 1 dl oil and season with salt. • Wash the marrows and, without removing the skins, cut them into thin slices and fry with the onions until they are transparent. Do not overfry to ensure that they do not disintegrate and lose their taste. • Remove the lightly fried vegetables and place in a colander to drain off any water. • Once well strained, heat in a non-stick frying pan with 1 dl oil. • Beat the eggs in a bowl, season and pour into the same frying pan as the marrows, mixing with care. • Reduce the heat so that the egg sets slowly. • Using a pan lid, flip the omelette so that it sets on the other side.

Presentation: When cool, cut the omelette into 6 portions and place on 6 slices of bread diagonally cut and previously spread with mayonnaise.

Tortilla de patatas
Potato omelette

- 1 kg potatoes
- 200 g onion, chopped
- 8 eggs, 50 g each

- 1 dl olive oil, maximum acidity 0.4°
- Salt

let's get started

Peel the potatoes and cut them into thin slices. • Heat the oil in a non-stick frying pan (25 cm in diameter) and add the potatoes. • Cook for 5 minutes then add the onion and salt. Maintain over a high heat and occasionally stir the potatoes with a spatula to make sure that they do not stick, moving them from the frying pan surface up to the top. When they are soft, strain them in a colander. • Mix the potatoes with the beaten eggs, stirring once and adding salt to taste. • Heat 3 tablespoons of the remaining oil in the frying pan and when it begins to smoke pour in the mixture. • Shake the frying pan gently so that the omelette does not stick and shape the edges using a skimmero Lower the heat and leave the omelette to set slowly. • When soft and juicy inside, flip on a plate and slide back into the frying pan to brown the other side for a few seconds.
Presentation: When cool, cut into portions.

Tortilla de pimientos del piquillo y bacalao
Piquillo (roasted red) pepper and cod omelette

- 100 g onion, chopped
- 400 g green peppers, chopped and de-seeded
- 3 cloves garlic

- 8 *piquillo* peppers, tinned
- 100 g crumbled cod
- 8 eggs
- 5 1/2 tablespoons oil

let's get started

Soak the cod for 12 hours, changing the water three times. • In a frying pan (20 cm in diameter) prepare a sauté by lightly frying the onion in oil. Once the onion is transparent, add the garlic and green peppers and fry until soft. Then add the red peppers and cod and lightly fry all ingredients together in 1/2 tablespoon of oil for 5 minutes, ensuring that the cod does not brown. Season. • Beat the eggs and add. Leave the omelette to fry on a very low heat. Once the omelette has set but is still juicy inside, flip over on a plate and slide back into the frying pan to brown and set on the other side.

Tortilla multicolor
Multi-coloured omelette

- 12 eggs (3 for each omelette)
- Olive oil and salt
- 1 x 150 g tin *atún claro* (tuna packed solid in oil)
- 2 tablespoons frozen spinach

- 100 g flat green beans
- 10 white asparagus tips, tinned
- 4 *piquillo* peppers, tinned and finely cut
- 3 tablespoons mayonnaise sauce

let's get started

Tuna omelette: Beat 3 eggs with salt and mix with crumbled tuna. Prepare a flat omelette in a frying pan (20 cm in diameter) with 3 tablespoons oil. • **Spinach and green bean omelette:** Cook the beans. Fry the spinach in 3 tablespoons oil and add the beans, beaten eggs and salt. Prepare the omelette. • **Asparagus omelette:** Heat the asparagus in the frying pan with 3 tablespoons oil and add the eggs and salt. Prepare the omelette. • **Pepper omelette:** Fry the peppers and add the eggs and salt. Prepare the omelette.
Presentation: Make a tower of omelettes alternating the colours and cover with mayonnaise.

fish and seafood

Almejas a la marinera
Clams in white wine sauce

- 1 kg clams
- 4 garlic cloves, chopped
- 1 dl olive oil
- 1 dl white wine
- 2 dl clam stock
- 2 tablespoons parsley, chopped
- 1 tablespoon flour
- Salt

let's get started

Shake the clams to remove any sand and soak in salted water. After 1/2 hour wash the clams and cook in 2 dl water. Remove the clams when they begin to open. • Strain the stock and set aside. • Lightly fry the garlic in the oil and, before it changes colour, add a tablespoon of flour dissolved in the wine and the clam stock. • When this liquid starts to boil, add the clams and sprinkle with parsley. Cook for 1 or 2 minutes.

Presentation: Arrange the clams in 6 individual dishes.

Anchoas marinadas
Marinated anchovies

- 15 anchovies
- Bread
- 1 teaspoon salt
- 1 tablespoon sugar
- 4 tablespoons red wine vinegar

- 10 tablespoons olive oil
- 1 laurel leaf, chopped
- 2 tablespoons chopped parsley
- 1 tablespoon chopped tarragon
- Ground pepper

let's get started

Prepare the pickle sauce or marinade by diluting the salt and sugar in the vinegar. Then add the other ingredients: oil, laurel, tarragon and a tablespoon of chopped parsley. • Remove the head and central bone from the anchovies. • Remove the fillets whole and place in a large dish (not a metal one). • Drizzle the fillets with pickle sauce and cover with cling film. Refrigerate the anchovies for 24 hours before serving.

Presentation: Cut the bread into 6 slices 1-cm thick. • Drizzle with a few drops of pickle sauce and then place the anchovy fillets on top. • Drizzle with another teaspoon of pickle sauce and sprinkle with the remaining chopped parsley.

Note: Maximum storage time 10 days.

Anchoas rellenas de pimientos
Anchovies stuffed with peppers

- 14 anchovies
- 3 tablespoons tinned tomato sauce
- 6 *ñoras* (dried peppers)
- 1 dl + 3 tablespoons olive oil
- 2 tablespoons bread crumbs
- 1/2 teaspoon sugar
- Salt
- 3 eggs
- Flour

let's get started

Wash the anchovies and remove the head and central bone. Lay the fillets out flat.
Stuffing: Crush the ñoras in an electric blender with 1 dl oil. • Fry the bread crumbs in three tablespoons of oil and add the oil from the ñoras, the tomato sauce, salt and a pinch of sugar.
• Spread an anchovy fillet with the stuffing and place another one on top to make a sandwich.
Final touches: Roll the anchovies in flour, beaten egg and then again in the flour. Fry in abundant oil.

Bacalao ahumado relleno de piperrada
Smoked cod stuffed with peppers and tomatoes

- 6 slices *chapata* (rustic-style bread)
- 6 fillets smoked cod
- 3 red peppers
- Strips of chives

PIPERRADA (PEPPERS AND TOMATOES):
- 2 tablespoons olive oil

- 100 g onion, chopped
- 2 green peppers, chopped
- 1 red pepper, tinned
- 2 garlic cloves, chopped
- 3 tablespoons tinned tomato purée

let's get started

Cover the red peppers in tinfoil and roast for 1 hour. • Leave to cool. • Peel and cut into 6 pieces. • **Piperrada:** Lightly fry the onion in oil; when transparent, add the garlic and green peppers. When all the ingredients are cooked, add 3 tablespoons of tomato purée.
Presentation: Lay out the 6 cod slices on the table. Stuff each slice with piperrada and make into a roll. Place half a red pepper on each slice of bread. • Top with the cod rolls and garnish with strips of chives.

Bocaditos de sardinas en aceite de oliva

Sardine snacks in olive oil

- 6 long *mediasnoches* (small bread buns)
- 6 tinned sardines in olive oil
- 12 teaspoons tomato sauce
- 1/2 onion, finely chopped
- 1 tomato

let's get started

Remove the skin from the sardines by gently scraping with a knife then remove the central bone, leaving only the fillets. • Place the tomato in boiling water for approximately 3 minutes then peel. Finely dice the tomato pulp. • Finely chop the onion.

Presentation: Cut the bread buns in half and drizzle with a few drops of sardine oil and tomato sauce. • Cover with the diced tomato and onion and top with the sardine fillets.

Bonito marinado en aceite de oliva
Atlantic bonito marinated in olive oil

- 6 slices *chapata* (rustic-style bread)
- 500 g Atlantic bonito
- 75 g bacon cut into strips and fried
- 6 teaspoons Maggi meat stock
- 1 tablespoon Pedro Ximénez sweet wine
- 3 tablespoons chopped onion
- 3 tablespoons grated Manchego cheese
- Virgin olive oil
- Salt
- Freshly ground pepper

let's get started

Freeze the bonito so that when hard it can be cut into very thin slices. Lay these slices in a dish then add salt and pepper and drizzle with the Pedro Ximénez wine and the meat stock. Cover with oil and leave to marinate for 1 to 2 hours.

Presentation: Lay the bonito slices on the pieces of bread. Add the cheese then sprinkle with the finely-chopped onion and bacon.

Boquerones en vinagre y sardinas
Fresh anchovies in vinegar and sardines

- 6 slices *chapata* (rustic-style bread)
- 1 kg fresh anchovies
- 6 large sardines
- 3 red peppers

MARINADE:
- 1 onion, finely chopped

- 2 garlic cloves, chopped
- 1 tablespoon aromatic herbs
- 8 black peppercorns
- 1/2 l oil
- 1 dl vinegar
- Salt and two tablespoons sugar

let's get started

Mix all the marinade ingredients. • Clean and fillet the anchovies. Place in the marinade and leave for two hours. • Clean the sardines using the same procedure. Arrange on a greased ovenproof tray, season and roast for 5 minutes at 170°. • Wrap the red peppers in tinfoil and roast for 50 minutes. Leave to cool in the foil then peel.

Presentation: Cover the bread slices with strips of red pepper. Lay the anchovies in vinegar on top and then, crosswise, the sardines.

Buñuelos de bacalao
Cod fritters

- 3/4 kg salted cod fillets

- Fritter dough (see recipe, p. 117)
- Abundant oil

let's get started

Soak the cod for 24 hours, changing the water approximately six times. Cook in cold water, removing from the water just before it begins to boil. Remove the bones and cut into equal pieces. • Prepare the fritter dough immediately prior to frying in order to serve hot. • Heat the oil in a large frying pan. Coat each piece of cod thoroughly in the fritter dough then fry until the dough is cooked inside.

Calamares pequeños en su tinta
Small squid in their ink

- 24 squids
- 1 onion, chopped
- 2 garlic cloves, chopped
- 1 green pepper, chopped
- Olive oil

- 2 dl tomato sauce (see recipe, p. 115)
- Squid ink or 3 small bags of ink
- Salt

let's get started

Clean the squid thoroughly, removing the very thin outer skin. Cut off the fins and remove the guts and bony cartilage. Set aside the tentacles and the small long bag containing the ink. Wash on the outside and turn inside out, as if it were a glove, and wash again. Chop up 6 whole squids and the tentacles and fins from the remaining ones. Lightly fry then stuff the remaining 18 squid with this mixture. • The sauce: Lightly fry the onion, garlic and pepper in the oil. When cooked, add the tomato sauce. Crush the ink bags with a little cooking salt and add a little water. • Cook the squid in this sauce until tender. • Add salt to taste.
Presentation: Arrange the squid in 6 individual dishes and serve hot.

Cazuelita de garbanzos, espinacas y bacalao

Chickpea, spinach and cod casserole

- 250 g chickpeas
- 1 whole onion, peeled
- 1 whole garlic bulb plus two garlic cloves, chopped
- 200 g spinach, frozen
- 150 g cod, salted and crumbled
- 1 dl olive oil
- Salt

let's get started

Soak the cod for 24 hours, changing the water several times. • Place the chickpeas in salted water the night before. Pour away this water and cook the chickpeas in 4 times their volume of water together with the onion and the whole garlic. When the chickpeas are almost tender, remove the onion and garlic and crush in the food mill. • Cover the base of a frying pan with oil and lightly fry the two chopped garlic cloves, adding the onion and garlic purée, spinach and cod. • Once lightly fried, return to the pan containing the chickpeas, add salt, and leave to cook until the chickpeas are tender.

Presentation: Arrange in 6 individual dishes.

Note: The exact cooking time cannot be specified since the quality of both chickpeas and water may vary. If you use a pressure cooker, check the chickpeas after 20 minutes.

Cocochas de bacalao

Cod cheeks

- 1 kg cod cheeks
- 4 tablespoons olive oil
- 6 tablespoons water
- 6 garlic cloves, chopped and without

shoots
- A few drops chili pepper oil or Tabasco
- 4 tablespoons parsley, chopped
- Salt

let's get started

Place the oil, chopped garlic and a pinch of salt in a large frying pan. Lightly fry over a low heat without browning and leave to cool completely. • Add the cod cheeks and season with a little salt. Gently shake the frying pan from side to side and gradually add approximately 6 tablespoons of water as the sauce begins to thicken. The exact amount of water required cannot be specified; the more added, the thinner the sauce. • Add the drops of chili pepper oil and parsley. Once well cooked, remove the cod cheeks from the heat.

Presentation: Arrange the cod cheeks and sauce in 6 individual dishes.

Note: Do not allow the sauce to boil whilst cooking the cod cheeks.

Chipirones encebollados
Cuttlefish and onions

SERVES TWO
- 6 small cuttlefish
- 3 spring onions, chopped
- 1 onion, cut into strips
- 1 leek (white portion), cut into strips
- Oil
- Salt

let's get started

Clean and gut the cuttlefish, removing the internal body cartilage. Wash and set aside the tentacles. Brown the cuttlefish on both sides in a frying pan with very hot oil. Season. Fry the tentacles separately, removing any excess liquid from the frying pan. • Lightly fry the spring onions, onion and leek in a little oil and season with salt. Arrange the vegetables on two plates and place the cuttlefish on top.

Note: Cuttlefish is a type of small squid that is born in summer and fished using bait. Recently caught squid must be left for 24 hours before cooking, otherwise it will be very hard.

Ensaladilla de marisco
Seafood salad

- 8 slices of *chapata* (rustic-style bread)
- 2 avocados
- 1 tin of *chatka* (Russian crabmeat)
- 1 kg prawns

- 200 g Iberian ham, sliced
- 1 lettuce and 1 lemon
- Mayonnaise sauce, readymade or homemade (see recipe, p. 116)

let's get started

Peel the avocados, cut into thick slices and drizzle with lemon juice. Cover with cling film and set aside. • Crumble the *chatka*. • Cook the prawns in salted water, making sure not to overcook. As soon as the prawns change colour, remove from the heat and peel. • Cut the ham into strips and fry until crispy. • Wash the lettuce well and then chop up and store in the refrigerator.

Presentation: Place the avocados and a little mayonnaise on the bread slices. Add the lettuce, *chatka* and prawns followed by more sauce and lettuce. Place the ham shavings in the centre.

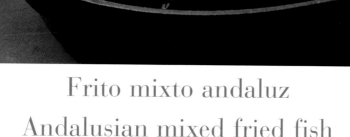

Frito mixto andaluz
Andalusian mixed fried fish

- One pomfret in fillets
- 250 g small red mullets
- 300 g *chopitos* or *puntillas* (baby squid)
- 250 g fresh anchovies
- 250 g squid rings
- Grain flour (special flour for frying fish)
- Salt

PICKLE SAUCE:
- 3 garlic cloves
- 2 laurel leaves
- 1 small glass white wine
- 1 tablespoon vinegar
- 1/4 l oil
- 2 tablespoons paprika
- Salt

let's get started

Remove the heads from the anchovies and pull the central bone through the exposed hole at the neck. If the anchovies are very small you do not need to remove the central bone. • Chop the pomfret fillets into small pieces and place in the pickle sauce, prepared using the ingredients listed above. • Season the fish that is not in pickle then roll in the flour and fry in very abundant hot oil. Drain on absorbent paper.

Presentation: Arrange on a plate, separating the different types of fish.

Gambas a la gabardina
Prawns in batter

- 1/2 kg prawns
- 2 l water
- 2 tablespoons sea salt
- 2 laurel leaves and salt

BATTER:
- 250 g flour

- 2 eggs
- 1 1/2 dl milk
- 2 tablespoons oil
- 1 teaspoon Royal yeast powder
- 1 teaspoon table salt
- Abundant oil for frying

let's get started

Add the laurel and salt to the water and heat. Bring to the boil and add the prawns for 2 1/2 minutes. They must only be half cooked. • Remove the heads from prawns and peel down to the tail. • Batter: Mix the flour with the yeast, add the beaten eggs, salt, oil and milk, stirring to make a consistent batter. • Roll each prawn, except for tail, in the batter and fry immediately. Make sure the oil is not too hot otherwise the prawns will be overcooked on the outside and undercooked on the inside.

Note: The cooking time for the prawns will depend on their weight. In this recipe we used prawns that weighed 25 g and there were 20 prawns in 1/2 kg.

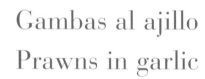

Gambas al ajillo
Prawns in garlic

- 300 g whole prawns
- 1 dl oil

- 5 garlic cloves, peeled and chopped
- 4 small pieces of chili pepper
- Salt

let's get started

Peel the prawns raw and set aside. • Pour the oil into a small pan and add the chopped garlic and chili peppers. Heat everything ensuring that the garlic does not brown then add the prawns and season moderately, stirring until the prawns change colour. Serve very hot.
Note: These amounts are for one individual portion.

Hígado de bacalao y huevas de salmón
Cod liver and salmon roe

- 1 tin 250 g cod liver
- 1 small tin salmon roe
- 6 rectangular cocktail toasts
- 1 branch of celery

- 2 tablespoons potato purée, in flakes
- 1 tablespoon oil
- Salt and nutmeg

let's get started

Store the cod liver very cold in the refrigerator. • **Purée:** Cook the celery branch in a pressure cooker for 15 minutes, strain the liquid and add the potato flakes, one tablespoon of oil and a small amount of the celery stock to make a thick potato purée.

Presentation: Arrange the purée into six portions and spread on the cocktail toasts. Place the cod liver on top and garnish with the salmon roe.

Marmitako

Basque-style tuna and potato stew

- 2 dl oil
- 2 onions, chopped
- 3 green peppers, chopped into rings
- 4 tinned *piquillo* peppers, chopped into small pieces
- 4 garlic cloves, chopped

- 2 kg potatoes
- 1 kg tuna
- 1 1/2 dl tomato purée (see recipe, p. 115)
- Salt and pepper
- 1 laurel leaf

let's get started

Fry the onions in the oil. Season with salt and add the garlic and green peppers. When almost fried, add the *piquillo* peppers. • Fry lightly then add the potatoes, previously chopped into medium-sized pieces. • Cover with water, add the tomato purée the laurel leaf, and leave to cook until tender. Add salt to taste. • Add the chopped tuna and leave to cook gently for approximately 15 minutes.

Presentation: Serve the stew in 6 individual dishes.

Mejillones rellenos fritos
Stuffed mussels

- 20 mussels
- 50 g butter
- 1 tablespoon olive oil, maximum acidity 0.4°
- 1/2 spring onion, chopped
- 50 g flour
- 3 dl milk
- 1 tablespoon white wine
- Salt
- Pepper

let's get started

Wash and scrape the mussel shells. Steam. Cover and when the water boils, leave until the shells open. Once the mussels have opened, remove the meat and set aside the shells.
Sauce: Melt the butter with a tablespoon of oil and lightly fry the chopped spring onion. Once transparent, add the flour. Then add the wine and milk to obtain a thick cream. Season. • Add the mussels and cook for a few seconds in the sauce then blend in an electric blender. Whilst this mixture is still hot, stuff the shells. Leave to cool then roll in the egg and bread crumbs and fry.

Merluza frita

Fried hake

- 6 slices *chapata* (rustic-style bread)
- 6 hake fillets, 100 g each
- 6 lettuce leaves
- 2 eggs
- Homemade mayonnaise sauce (see recipe, p. 116)
- Flour for batter
- Salt
- Abundant oil for frying

let's get started

Ask your fishmonger to cut six fillets from the central part of the hake. • Season and roll in egg and flour. Fry in abundant oil until a crust forms, then lower the heat so that they cook inside. **Presentation:** Pour a tablespoon of mayonnaise on each slice of bread, then top with a lettuce leaf and some more mayonnaise. Finally, top with the fried hake fillet.

Picadillo de mariscos con salsa rosa
Seafood cocktail

- 6 slices *chapata* (rustic-style bread)
- 1 kg monkfish (central part), diced
- 10 crab sticks, chopped
- 300 g king prawns, peeled

- 6 scallops
- 4 dl cocktail sauce (see recipe, p. 116)
- 2 tablespoons oil, salt and pepper

let's get started

If you buy the monkfish frozen, it will shrink until it weighs about 400 gr. There will be less loss with fresh monkfish. Place in a sieve and submerge in a saucepan with boiling water until it cooks. Set aside in a bowl. • Peel the prawns and cook in the same way as the monkfish and set aside in the same bowl. • Chop up the crab sticks and add to the other ingredients. • Open the scallop shells and remove the blackish film. • Separate the coral, taking care not to break it, and fry in a little oil. Set aside separately for the garnish. Chop up the white scallop meat and cook lightly. Add to the same bowl. • Stir 3 dl of cocktail sauce into the fish and add salt and pepper to taste.

Presentation: Arrange this mixture on the bread slices. Use the remaining sauce to make rosettes, place these on the bread slices and top with the scallop coral.

Pulpo a la gallega
Galicia-style octopus

- 2 packets cooked octopus
- 2 tablespoons paprika
- 1 cube fish stock

- 2 laurel leaves
- Sea salt for sprinkling the octopus
- 1 teaspoon sea salt for the stock
- 2 dl olive oil

let's get started

Place the octopus for 15 minutes in a stock prepared using the stock cube, laurel leaves and salt. Remove with a skimmer, drain well and arrange on a plate.

Presentation: Sprinkle the octopus with salt and paprika and drizzle with oil. Add more paprika.

Note: If the octopus is purchased raw, it must be cooked for 3 hours with laurel and a bottle cork then left to cool in the cooking liquid.

Salpicón de mariscos
Seafood salad

- 1 spring onion, chopped into strips
- 1 1/2 kg prawns, weighing 50 g each
- 1 kg mussels

- 3 large red shrimps
- 1 dl virgin olive oil
- 2 tablespoons sherry vinager
- Salt
- Laurel

let's get started

Boil 1 litre of water with 40 g of salt and two laurel leaves. Once the water is boiling fiercely, add the prawns and large red shrimps. The prawns must cook for 90 seconds and the large red shrimps for 1 or 2 minutes more (depending on their size). Remove from the pan as they cook and leave to cool. Once cold, peel and chop into pieces. • Wash the mussel shells thoroughly, place in a frying pan with a small amount of water and cook. When the mussels open, remove the meat from their shells. • Prepare a vinaigrette dressing by dissolving the salt in the vinegar and whisking with the oil. Add the spring onion and seafood. It is best left for a few hours before serving.

Setas y gambas gratinadas
Mushroom and prawn bake

- 3 bread rolls (6 cm in diameter)
- 4 tablespoons olive oil
- 4 garlic cloves, chopped
- 300 g mushrooms or wild mushrooms
- 150 g bacon, cut into strips
- 200 g peeled prawns
- 1 1/2 dl cream
- 6 tablespoons grated cheese
- 6 teaspoons chopped parsley
- Salt and pepper

let's get started

Fry the bacon in the oil. As soon as it begins to turn crispy, add the garlic and sliced mushrooms. When fried, add the cream and simmer to reduce the liquid. • Add the prawns and when cooked remove from the heat.

Presentation: Cut the bread rolls in half. Pour some of the juice onto the bread then divide the sauté amongst the slices. Sprinkle with cheese and brown in the oven. • Finally, add the chopped parsley.

Tapa de patatas y salmón ahumado
Potato with smoked salmon

- 1 *chapata* (rustic-style bread)
- 3 potatoes, peeled and chopped into slices 1-cm thick
- 3 slices smoked salmon
- 6 tablespoons mayonnaise, readymade or homemade (see recipe, p. 116)
- 1 teaspoon dried dill
- 1 natural yoghurt

let's get started

Add a tablespoon of yoghurt and the dill to the mayonnaise. • Place the potatoes in salted water, bring to the boil and simmer.

Presentation: Cut 6 slices of bread. Spread with mayonnaise, add 2 or 3 slices of boiled potato, spread again with mayonnaise and top with half a slice of salmon.

Tapa de salmón y espárragos trigueros
Salmon with wild asparagus

- **6 slices *chapata* (rustic-style bread)**
- **3 slices smoked salmon**

- **30 wild asparagus shoots**
- **6 chive stalks**
- **Smoked sauce (see recipe, p. 115)**

let's get started

Cook the spring onion in a microwave for 1 minute or in a saucepan for 2 minutes with a little water. • Cut the asparagus shoots down to 8 cm. Tie them into two bunches and cook in boiling salted water with the tips pointing upwards. Once they are "al dente", remove from the pan and submerge in another pan of very cold water. Remove and untie the two bunches. Make small bunches of 5 asparagus shoots each, using the chive stalks to tie them.
Presentation: Cut the bread into long slices, spread with sauce and top with salmon rolled in olive oil. Finally, add the bunches of asparagus.

Tapa de sardinas y mejillones
Sardines with mussels

SARDINE PATÉ:
- 1 tin (150 g) sardines in olive oil
- 1 tin (150 g) mussels in pickle sauce
- 50 g Philadelphia cheese
- 50 g butter

PEPPER SAUCE:
- 1 red pepper
- 1 dl cream
- Salt and pepper

- Rectangular cocktail toasts

let's get started

Pepper sauce: Wrap one red pepper in tinfoil and roast in the oven at 160°. After one hour, turn off the oven and leave the pepper to cool in its wrapping before peeling. • Place half of the roasted pepper in the electric blender. Add the cream, salt and black pepper, and blend.
• **Sardine paté:** Remove the central bone, blend the sardines with the cheese and soft butter.
Presentation: Spread the cocktail toasts with the pepper sauce. Using two teaspoons of paté, make a croquette and place on top of the toasts. • Top with a mussel in pickle sauce.

Tartaletas de gulas
Baby eel tartlets

59

- 6 pastry tartlets, readymade or homemade (see recipe, p. 118)
- 200 g baby eels
- 2 dl olive oil

- 3 garlic cloves, chopped
- 2 chili peppers, chopped into small pieces
- Salt (very little)

let's get started

First prepare the tartlets. Regardless of whether they are made from homemade or frozen pastry, this must be rolled out properly and very thin. Once the tartlets have been baked, leave to cool and remove from the baking tin. • Sprinkle the baby eels with a little salt and arrange lengthwise in a deep dish. Meanwhile, fry the garlic and chili peppers in a frying pan. When the oil boils, pour the contents of the frying pan over the baby eels, stirring so that they are all thoroughly coated in oil. They must remain succulent.

Presentation: Fill the tartlets with the baby eels and serve very hot.

Meat and Poultry

Albóndigas
Meatballs

- 500 g beef, minced
- 3 sausages
- 40 g smoked belly pork
- 4 pieces of sliced bread
- 1 dl cream
- 2 eggs
- 1 garlic clove, finely chopped
- 1 tablespoon parsley

- Flour and salt

SAUCE:
- 1 onion, chopped
- 1 carrot, finely chopped
- 1/2 tomato, peeled and chopped
- 1 tablespoon toasted flour
- 2 dl oil
- 1 (cube) meat stock and salt

let's get started

Ask your butcher to mince the belly pork and beef together. Skin the sausages and add the meat to the minced meat mixture. • Soak the bread in the cream and pour into the blender together with the eggs, salt, chopped garlic and parsley. Blend the mixture and add to the meat. Knead together, shape into balls then roll in the flour. Fry the balls in very hot oil until they are crusty on the outside. • **Sauce:** Lightly fry the onion until transparent then add the carrot, tomato and salt. Add the toasted flour, 2 glasses of water and one meat stock cube. Cook for 30 minutes and put through a food mill. • Heat the meatballs in the sauce for 15 to 20 minutes.

Brocheta de solomillo ibérico adobado
Marinated Iberian sirloin brochette

- 1 sirloin steak (300 g)

MARINADE:
- 1/2 onion, chopped into strips
- 2 garlic cloves, chopped
- 1 laurel leaf, chopped
- 1 tablespoon aromatic herbs

- 2 tablespoons cayenne pepper
- 1 tablespoon soya sauce
- 1 dl sherry vinegar
- 1 glass olive oil
- Salt
- Freshly-ground pepper

let's get started

Prepare the marinade by mixing all the ingredients. • Remove the fatty tissue and nerves from the sirloin, dice and leave to stand in the marinade for a few hours.

Presentation: Place 3 dices of meat on each wooden skewer and fry quickly in oil.

Caldereta de cordero

Lamb stew

- 1 kg lamb, chopped
- 2 onions, finely chopped
- 2 green peppers, chopped
- 1 dl olive oil
- 12 small new potatoes, peeled
- 4 garlic cloves
- 3 laurel leaves

- 2 tablespoons fresh parsley, chopped
- 1 tablespoon paprika
- 1 teaspoon sea salt
- Freshly-ground pepper
- 1 tablespoon red wine vinegar
- 1 heaped tablespoon flour

let's get started

Lightly fry the onions and peppers in the oil. Add the pieces of lamb, previously lightly seasoned with salt. Sauté the mixture for a few seconds. • Crush the garlic, laurel, parsley, paprika, salt and pepper and dissolve everything in the vinegar and a little water. Pour over the stew and cover completely with water. • After half an hour add the potatoes and leave until everything is cooked. Add the flour dissolved in a little water to thicken the sauce and bring to the boil.
Presentation: Arrange in 6 individual dishes and serve very hot.

Callos a la madrileña
Madrid-style tripe

- 1 1/2 kg tripe
- 1/2 kg snout, chopped
- 1 cow's foot, de-boned and chopped into pieces
- 200 g Serrano ham
- 8 dried peppers
- 100 g soft chorizo sausage (mildly cured)

- 1 *morcilla* (Spanish black pudding) (optional)
- Salt and peppercorns
- 1 dl olive oil
- 2 onions, chopped
- 4 garlic cloves, chopped
- 1 cup tomato sauce (see recipe, p. 115)

- 2 cups tripe stock
- 1 small piece of chili pepper or a few drops of Tabasco

let's get started

Place the tripe and chopped snout in water with a good splash of vinegar and the sea salt. After one hour wash in cold water. • Cook in a pressure cooker with water and add the ham, dried peppers and approximately 15 black peppercorns. After 45 minutes check the cooking point and add the chorizo sausage and, if you like it this way, the *morcilla*. Cook for another 20 minutes. • To make the sauce, lightly fry the onion and garlic in oil. When transparent, add the tomato sauce, tripe stock and chili. Once cooked, put through a food mill and pour over the tripe and snout. Add the chorizo sausage and *morcilla* (if included), cut into slices.

Canapé de chorizo de Pamplona
Pamplona chorizo sausage canapé

- 6 pieces sliced bread
- 6 slices Manchego cheese
- 6 slices Pamplona chorizo sausage
- 6 eggs

- 3 tablespoons cream
- 6 tablespoons olive oil
- 50 g green noodles
- Salt

let's get started

Noodles: Cook the noodles until they are "al dente", drain and sauté in one tablespoon of oil.

Omelettes: Beat the eggs with the cream and a pinch of salt. Heat the oil in a frying pan (7 cm in diameter) and make the 6 omelettes.

Presentation: Place an omelette on each slice of bread, then one slice of cheese and finally the chorizo sausage. Trim with a pasta cutter to create a round shape. Garnish with the omelette scraps and the noodles.

Chistorra con queso gratinada
Spicy sausage and cheese bake

- 250 g spicy sausage
- 6 slices of Emmental cheese

let's get started

Cut the sausage into 2-cm pieces and place an equal amount in 6 ramekin dishes. • Cover the sausage with the cheese slices and bake in the oven until the cheese melts.

Chuletitas de cordero con besamel

Lamb cutlets in béchamel sauce

- 6 lamb cutlets
- Béchamel sauce (see recipe, p. 114)

BATTER:
- Eggs, beaten
- Flour
- Breadcrumbs

let's get started

Remove the cartilage from the lamb cutlets. Season with salt and fry in the oil. The meat should remain pink. • Prepare the béchamel sauce according to the recipe, but using 60 g of flour instead of 30 g. • Dip the cutlets one by one in hot béchamel sauce and leave to cool on a greased tray. Once cold, roll in flour, eggs and bread and then fry in abundant oil.

Empanadillas de carne

Meat pasties

- Frozen puff pastry or homemade pasty pastry (see recipe, p. 118)
- 200 g roast or stewed meat
- 1 dl tomato sauce (p. 115)
- A few drops of Worcestershire sauce (Perrins)
- A few drops of Tabasco (optional)
- 1 egg, beaten
- Salt

let's get started

Mince the meat in an electric blender and mix with the tomato sauce and Perrins sauce. For a more spicy taste, add a few drops of Tabasco. Season with salt. • Roll out the pastry and cut into circles (7 cm in diameter). Add stuffing to each circle and close, sealing the edges with a little beaten egg and pressing down on them with a fork. • Fry in abundant oil.
Note: The pastry can be prepared in advance but the pasties must be fried freshly stuffed.

Hígado de pato con cebolla confitada
Duck liver with caramelized onions

- *Chapata* (rustic-style bread)
- Fresh duck liver
- 2 dl sweet Pedro Ximénez wine
- Salt and freshly-ground pepper
- 1 kg onion, chopped into strips
- 100 g butter
- 2 tablespoons olive oil, maximum acidity 0.4°
- 160 g sugar
- 1/4 l red wine
- 1 dl Módena vinegar
- Salt

let's get started

Onion caramel: Take a thick-based non-stick saucepan. Melt the butter with the oil then add the onion. Fry for five minutes then pour in the red wine and vinegar, adding the sugar and a little salt. Leave to simmer until all the liquid has evaporated. • Boil the sweet Pedro Ximénez wine until half has evaporated. • **Duck liver:** Soak the duck liver in cold water for 12 hours. Remove any traces of bile and blood. • Separate the two lobes and remove the veins using a cloth. Cut into fillets. • Fry the liver fillets in their own fat, leaving them fairly rare.
Presentation: Place the onion caramel on the bread, top with the liver and drizzle with the remaining sweet Pedro Ximénez wine. This recipe makes approximately 15 tapas.

Lomo adobado y manzanas caramelizadas
Marinated pork with caramelized apples

- 6 pieces sliced bread
- 6 marinated loin of pork fillets (275 g)
- 3 Golden Delicious apples (approx. 250 g)
- Olive oil for frying the fillets

- 75 g sugar for caramelizing the apples sand 2 tablespoons more for the apple purée
- Salt

let's get started

Fry the lion of pork fillets without any seasoning. • Peel one apple and cut into 12 fairly equal segments. Line a pan and add enough water to cover them. Boil and when soft drain off almost all the water. Add the sugar and heat until it begins to caramelize. Remove the apple slices from the pan whilst still hot and place on each pork fillet. • Boil the remaining 2 apples in water and sugar and then blend to a purée.

Presentation: Cover each slice of bread with apple purée and top with a pork fillet and caramelised apple.

Note: We recommend purchasing Iberian marinated loin of pork. Although a little more expensive, it is not only more aromatic but also more tender.

Morcilla de Burgos con manzana

Burgos *morcilla* (Spanish black pudding) with apples

- **1 Burgos *morcilla* (blood sausage)**
- **2 pippin apples**

- **1 lemon**
- **French bread (baguette)**

let's get started

Dice one apple and cut the other one into thin segments. Drizzle with a few drops of lemon juice.
• Skin the *morcilla* and chop up lightly to separate the small pieces of meat. Heat a frying pan
without oil and add the *morcilla* mixed with the diced apple. As soon as the fruit is cooked,
remove from the heat.
Presentation: Cut the bread into slices and top each slice with the *morcilla*. • Garnish with the
apple segments.

Morcilla de Burgos con pimiento verde

Burgos *morcilla* (Spanish black pudding) with green peppers

- 6 slices *chapata* (rustic-style bread)
- 3 green peppers
- 2 Burgos *morcillas*
- Olive oil

---

let's get started

Cut the peppers in two lengthwise and the *morcillas* into slices 2-cm thick. • Fry the peppers in a frying pan coated with oil until they are tender "al dente". Remove then fry the *morcilla*.
Presentation: Cut the bread into diagonal slices. Place 1/2 green pepper and one slice of *morcilla* on each piece of bread.

Plato de Jabugo
Plate of Jabugo ham

- **6 slices *lacón* (shoulder ham)**
- **6 slices Jabugo ham**
- **12 slices Jabugo fillets**

- **12 slices Jabugo chorizo sausage**
- **Bread sticks**

let's get started

The only effort involved in this recipe is buying good sausage and ham, which will be expensive.
This exquisite, unique and essentially Spanish dish is gaining fans around the world.
Presentation: Separate the different types of sausage and ham into four sections and arrange on a
serving plate around a pile of bread sticks.

Pollo al ajillo

Chicken in garlic

- 1 chicken, chopped
- 3 garlic cloves, chopped
- 6 garlic cloves, unpeeled
- 1/2 dl dry sherry
- 2 dl olive oil
- Salt

let's get started

Rub the chicken pieces with the chopped garlic and salt. • Place the oil in an earthernware casserole dish and as soon as it is warm, add the chicken and unpeeled garlic and brown. Add the wine and boil until it evaporates.

Presentation: Serve in the same earthernware casserole dish as the one in which it has been cooked.

Rabo de buey

Oxtail

- **2 oxtails, chopped**
- **4 onions, chopped**
- **2 carrots, sliced**
- **6 garlic cloves, crushed**
- **2 dl olive oil**

- **2 tablespoons brandy**
- **3 turns of a black pepper mill**
- **Red wine to cover the oxtail**
- **Salt**

let's get started

Place the oxtails in a casserole dish just large enough to hold them. • Separately, lightly fry the onions in the oil and when transparent add the garlic and carrots. Season with salt and pepper and pour over the oxtails. Add the brandy and enough red wine to amply cover the oxtail. Cover the casserole dish. • Heat and when it begins to boil fiercely, place in an oven at 100°. After 4 hours, check that the oxtails are tender, remove and arrange on a plate. Remove the grease from the stock left in the casserole dish and pour over the oxtails. • Serve very hot.

Note: Oxtails can be prepared in a pressure cooker for 40 minutes but there is a risk that they may overcook, so cooking must be controlled carefully.

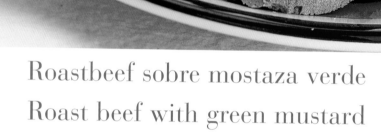

Roastbeef sobre mostaza verde
Roast beef with green mustard

- 1 1/2 kg rump
- 1 tin green mustard
- 6 slices *chapata* (rustic-style bread)

- 1 pickled gherkin
- Olive oil
- Salt and pepper

let's get started

In order to obtain 6 thin slices of meat, you will need to roast 1 kg or 1 1/2 kg. Season and drizzle with oil. • Roast 20 minutes per kg on the rack at 190°. Once roasted, leave to cool then cut into 6 thin slices.

Presentation: Spread each slice of bread with mustard. Roll up the roast beef slices and place on the bread, decorating with a slice of pickled gherkin.

Note: Use the remaining roast beef for other dishes.

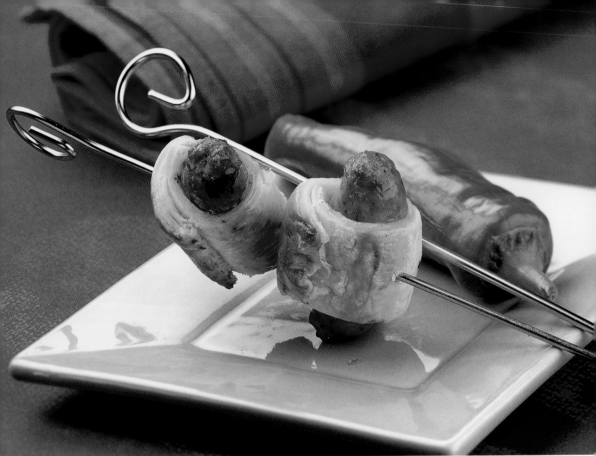

Salchichitas en hojaldre
Sausage rolls

- **12 small sausages**
- **1 layer of frozen puff-pastry**
- **Mild mustard**

- **1/2 l white wine**
- **1 egg, beaten**

let's get started

Pierce the sausages so that they do not burst when cooked and boil in the wine. Leave to cool completely and then spread with mustard. • Roll out the pastry with care and cut into strips that are slightly narrower than the sausages. • Wrap the sausages in the pastry, using the beaten egg to seal the edges and brush the pastry. Bake in the oven at 180° for 20-25 minutes.

Presentation: Garnish with *Guernica* (Biscay-style) peppers.

Note: You can use other small sausages such as cocktail *choricitos* or *chistorras* (both types of spicy sausage).

Solomillo ibérico con salsa de pimientos
Iberian pork in pepper sauce

- 6 slices French bread (baguette)
- 6 Iberian loin of pork fillets
- 3 *piquillo* peppers, tinned

- 1 dl cream
- Salt and pepper

let's get started

Season the fillets and fry in olive oil. • Cook the *piquillo* peppers with the cream in a small saucepan and season with salt and pepper. As soon as they begin to boil, remove and grind in an electric blender.

Presentation: Spread the bread slices with a little pepper sauce. Place the fillets on top and cover with more sauce.

Solomillo ibérico y queso azul

Iberian loin of pork and blue cheese

- 6 slices French bread (baguette)
- 150 g Iberian loin of pork fillets
- 50 g onion, very finely chopped
- 4 tablespoons olive oil

- 100 g blue cheese from Asturias
- 100 g cheese spread, e.g. Philadelphia
- Salt

let's get started

Fry the onion very well in 3 tablespoons of oil. • Soften the cheeses for 1 minute in an oven and blend together using a fork. Place in a pastry bag with a nozzle 1/2 cm in diameter. • Season the 6 fillets and brown in the remaining tablespoon of oil.

Presentation: Arrange the onion on the 6 slices of bread. Place the fillets on the bread slices and top each with a cheese rosette.

Tapa de cebollitas glaseadas y foiegras de pollo
Glazed shallots and chicken foie gras

- 6 slices toasted bread with oil, garlic and parsley

FOIE GRAS:
- 250 g chicken liver
- 75 g butter
- 1 tablespoon *oloroso* sherry
- 1 tablespoon aromatic herbs

- 1 teaspoon sugar
- Salt and pepper

CARAMELIZED SHALLOTS:
- 10 French shallots
- 100 g sugar
- 2 tablespoons oil
- 3 dl water, salt

let's get started

Foie gras: Clean the livers, removing any traces of green bile. Place in a saucepan with the butter, sherry, herbs, salt, sugar and pepper. Cook until the butter melts and the livers turn pinkish. Crush in an electric blender. • **Shallots:** Place 100 g of sugar in a saucepan and a few drops of lemon. Heat until the sugar caramelizes. Add the French shallots to the same saucepan. Submerge them in caramel, then cover with water and a good splash of oil. Sprinkle with a little salt and leave to simmer until the water is absorbed.
Presentation: Place shallots and a foie gras rosette side by side on each slice of bread.

Tapa de foiegras, aguacate y jamón de pato
Foie gras, avocado and duck ham

- 6 slices French bread
  (baguette)
- 100 g tin or jar of duck foie
  gras mousse

- 50 g duck ham, vacuum-wrapped
- 1 avocado

let's get started

Heat the plastic bag containing the duck in hot water. This allows you to open the bag and makes it easy to separate the slices. • Peel the avocado and then cut in half lengthwise; the large stone will remain encrusted in one of the halves; in order not to spoil the pulp, pierce the bone using a knife so that it can be easily removed. Cut the pulp into small slices 1/2 cm thick.

Presentation: Spread the slices of bread with foie gras, 2 slices of avocado, the duck in the centre and then another 2 slices of avocado.

Tartaletas de picadillo de chorizo
Diced chorizo sausage tartlets

- 1/2 kg diced pork or 1 kg fresh chorizo sausage
- 6 slices of *chapata* (rustic-style bread)

let's get started

Place the diced pork or chorizo stuffing in a hot frying pan, without any fat, and stir until the meat is cooked.

Presentation: Cover the bread with hot stuffing and serve.

Note: Diced pork is the ready-chopped meat used to make chorizo sausages. In many parts of the Spanish region of Castile, it can be bought as a stuffing. If you cannot find it in this form, you can make it by buying fresh uncured chorizo and removing the meat from the skin.

Miscellaneous

Buñuelos de queso

Cheese puffs

- Batter for puffs (see recipe, p. 117)
- 2 leeks

CHEESE CREAM:
- 100g Roquefort or Asturias cheese
- 50g butter
- 100g Philadelphia cheese

let's get started

Cheese cream: Gently heat the cheeses and butter to that they easier to work with. Blend together, stirring vigorously to obtain a consistent cream. **Leeks:** Separate the layers, cut into thin strips and fry until crunchy.

Presentation: Stuff the puffs, which you will have made beforehand, with the cheese cream and arrange on a round plate. Garnish with the fried leek.

Canutillos de jamón y queso
Ham and cheese rolls

- 6 thin slices cooked ham
- 6 slices Gruyère cream cheese
- 1 dl cream
- 50g butter
- 2 tablespoons strong creamy cheese
- 1 tablespoon potato purée, in flakes

TO COAT IN EGG AND BREAD CRUMBS:
- 2 eggs
- Bread crumbs
- Olive oil for frying

let's get started

Heat the cream together with the creamy cheese and butter. As soon as it boils, add the purée flakes. Stir continuously over the heat to obtain a thick purée. • Lay out a slice of ham and cover with a slice of cheese and a little hot purée. Roll up and secure with two toothpicks. • Once the purée has cooled, coat the rolls with egg and bread crumbs and fry in abundant oil.

Coca de sobrasada
Spicy pork sausage quiche

FILLING:
- 200g *sobrasada* (spicy pork sausage)
- 2 tablespoons instant onion soup
- 1 tablespoon Pedro Ximénez sweet wine
- 1 tablespoon sugar

PASTRY:
- 1 dl oil
- 1/2 dl white wine
- 2 eggs
- 20g baker's yeast
- 1 tablespoon salt and 1/2 tablespoon sugar
- 300g flour

let's get started

The pastry: Dilute the yeast in lukewarm white wine. Add the oil and beaten eggs. Stir and add the flour mixed with the salt and sugar. Knead for 10 minutes to obtain an elastic consistency. Roll out the pastry with a rolling pin, making a circle and pinching the border with your fingers to raise the edges and increase the capacity of the quiche. Pierce the interior with a fork.
• **Filling:** Gently heat the sobrasada. Add the sweet wine and onion soup and stir to obtain a consistent blend. • Fill the quiche lining with the stuffing then cover with tinfoil and bake in the oven at 180° for 25 minutes. Half-way through the cooking time, remove the foil and check regularly to make sure that the surface does not toast.
Note: The pastry indicated above can be replaced by frozen puff-pastry.

Crêpes rellenas de ensalada de pollo
Chicken salad pancakes

- Batter for pancakes (p. 117)
- 1 large cup of finely-chopped lettuce
- 2 creamy yoghurts
- 1 chicken breast
- A few drops of Worcestershire sauce (Perrins)

- 1 meat stock cube
- Salt
- A few sprigs of parsley
- A few strips of pepper

let's get started

Prepare the pancakes as indicated in the recipe or buy readymade. • Cook the chicken breast for 12 minutes in boiling water with the meat stock cube then chop finely. • Wash the lettuce and chop into tiny pieces. • Mix the yoghurt with a few drops of Worcestershire (Perrins) sauce and season. • Mix the finely chopped chicken with the yoghurt sauce and lettuce. Stuff the pancakes, roll up and garnish with parsley and pepper.

Croquetas de pollo y jamón
Chicken and ham croquettes

- Béchamel sauce (see recipe, p. 114)
- 150g roast or boiled chicken
- 30g ham
- Salt
- Nutmeg

let's get started

Prepare the béchamel sauce using 60g flour and the same amounts of the other ingredients as indicated in the recipe. Add the chicken and ham, mixing well. Bring to the boil then leave to cool completely, covering the surface with cling film to prevent a crust from forming. • Using two spoons, make small elongated shapes out of the mixture for the croquettes. Brush with beaten egg and roll in bread crumbs. Shape the croquettes again. Fry in the oil at 170°.

Note: The amounts given for the flour and milk are approximate since the flour will absorb more or less liquid depending on its degree of moisture. The béchamel sauce must nevertheless remain thick.

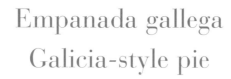

Empanada gallega
Galicia-style pie

FILLING:
- 2 dl oil and salt
- 3 onions, chopped
- 4 *piquillo* peppers, bottled
- 1 tomato, peeled and chopped
- 3 tins sardines in oil or 1 kg fresh sardines

PASTRY:
- 500 g flour
- 1 1/2 dl oil
- 1/2 dl cream or milk
- 2 eggs, 1 beaten egg
- 1 tablespoon salt, 1 tablespoon sugar
- 30 g baker's yeast

let's get started

Filling: Lightly fry the onions and peppers in the oil. • Scrape the skin from the sardines and remove the central bone. Add to the onion sauté. Once transparent, add the tomato and salt. Fry everything lightly until it is well done. • **Pastry:** Dilute the yeast in the warm cream or milk. Add the wine, oil and beaten eggs. Add the flour, salt and sugar. Knead by hand or in an electric blender for 10 minutes until the pastry acquires an elastic consistency. • Once the pastry is ready, divide into two parts. Roll out one half with a rolling pin and cover with the sautéd ingredients. Then cover with the other sheet of pastry. Brush the surface with beaten egg and bake in the oven at 180° for 25 minutes.

Fideuá

Fish and seafood stew

- 250g thick noodles
- 2 green peppers
- 4 garlic cloves
- 1/2 kg squid
- 1/2 kg prawns

- 1 dl olive oil
- 3/4 l fish stock
- Salt
- *Alioli* sauce (see recipe, p. 114)

let's get started

Heat the oven to 250°. Fry the prawns in a frying pan with oil for a few minutes and then peel. Boil the prawn heads then grind them in a food mill. Set the stock aside. • Sauté the garlic, peppers and squid in a *paellera* (special frying pan for making paella); then add the noodles and stir until they are well sautéd. • Pour in the boiling prawn stock, adding water if necessary. • Bake in the oven for 20 minutes. Add the prawns at the end.
Presentation: Serve with *alioli* sauce.

Migas con jamón y chorizo
Breadcrumbs with ham and chorizo sausage

- 1 round white bread (500 g)
- 3 garlic cloves
- 2 tablespoons paprika
- 4 tablespoons water
- 3 tablespoons oil
- 50g Serrano ham, diced
- 12 small slices of chorizo

let's get started

It is best to prepare the breadcrumbs the night before. Crumble the bread without the crust.
• Chop up the garlic and mix with the water and paprika. Soak the breadcrumbs in this mixture, stirring thoroughly to ensure that all the bread crumbs are coated equally. Roll the crumbs into a ball, wrap in a damp cloth and leave to stand for 12 hours. • Fry the breadcrumbs in a little oil. Toast, making sure that they do not become too greasy. • Flatten out the bread crumbs, make a space in the middle and add the ham and chorizo. Eat freshly made.

Paella

- 2 large cups of rice
- 300g prawns
- 100g lean pork, diced
- 10 chicken wings
- 1 1/2 dl olive oil
- 3 garlic cloves

- 1 tomato, peeled and chopped
- A few drops of lemon juice
- Salt and saffron
- 4 large cups prawn stock

- 2 hard-boiled eggs and 1 pepper, tinned

UTENSIL: 1 *paellera* (large frying pan used for making paella)

let's get started

Peel the prawns, fry the tails for a few seconds and store in the refrigerator. Boil the heads in water for 30 minutes, grind and drain using a food mill. Set the hot stock aside, leaving on the heat. Season the meat with salt and pepper. Sauté the garlic, chicken and pork with oil in the *paellera*. Add the rice, stirring for 5 minutes. • Add the lemon juice, tomato, salt, pepper and crushed saffron. Pour in the hot prawn stock, adding more water if necessary. Bring to the boil and then bake in the cook at 180° for 20 minutes and leave to stand for another 15 minutes outside the oven. If the rice is still hard and dry, sprinkle with a little water and cover and cook for a few more minutes.

Presentation: Garnish with the fried prawns, hard-boiled eggs and peppers.

Pincho de diversos escabeches
Assorted pickled skewer

- 6 pieces of round wholemeal bread
- 1 tin tomato purée
- 3 quail eggs
- 1 tin mussels in brine
- 1 tin olives stuffed with red pepper
- 1 tin picked onions
- 1 *piquillo* pepper, finely chopped
- 6 gherkins

let's get started

Spread the bread with the tomato sauce. • Cut each gherkin into 4 pieces and place face to face on each slice. Place the mussels, onions and pepper alternately at the angles formed by the gherkins. Finish off with half a quail egg, previously boiled for 5 minutes, at the centre.

Queso de cabra sobre cebolla
Goat's cheese and onion

- 6 slices chapata (rustic-style bread)
- 6 portions goat's cheeses
- 1 onion, chopped
- 2 cloves garlic, chopped
- 3 tablespoons olive oil
- Malaga raisins

let's get started

Cut the bread diagonally to make larger slices. • Lightly fry the onion and when it becomes transparent add the garlic taking care that it does not toast. • Slice the goat's cheese portions in half. • Place the onion sauté and any oil remaining in the frying pan on the bread and cover with two halves of cheese. • Heat in the oven at 160° for a couple of minutes to soften the cheese.

Presentation: Top with the raisins.

Queso frito de cabra
Fried goat's cheese

- 6 pieces of sliced bread
- 1 ripe fleshy tomato
- 6 teaspoons virgin olive oil
- 2 portions goat's cheese
- 80 g bread crumbs

- 2 tablespoons paprika
- A pinch of sugar
- 2 eggs for batter
- 3 pickled gherkins

let's get started

Cut the bread into round slices the size of the tomato. • Cut the tomato into very thin slices. • Cut each cheese portion into 3 slices. • Mix the bread crumbs with the paprika. • Finally, roll the cheese in the egg and bread crumbs and fry.

Presentation: Place one slice of tomato on each slice of bread. Sprinkle with a pinch of sugar and drizzle with a teaspoon of oil. Top with the fried cheese and garnish with gherkin.

Queso, higos y jamón de bellota
Cheese, figs and ham

- 6 pieces of sliced bread
- 6 tablespoons virgin olive oil

- 100g *bellota* ham (ham from acorn-fed pigs), very thinly sliced
- 100g creamy cheese
- 6 figs

let's get started

Cut the bread into round slices and toast. • Open the figs into four to make a flower. • Spread the bread with the oil and then with the cheese. Top with the ham and figs.

Tip: It is best to buy more figs than the number required for the recipe because some spoil when cut.

Sobrasada y torta del Casar gratinada
Spicy pork sausage and ewe's milk cheese au gratin

- 6 pieces of *chapata* (rustic-style bread)
- 6 slices of *sobrasada* (spicy pork sausage)

- 1 *torta del Casar* cheese (ewe's milk cheese)

let's get started

Cut the bread diagonally into long slices. • Buy one softish *torta del Casar* and remove the top cover with a knife to leave the cheese cream exposed. • Cover the bread with the *sobrasada* and approximately 2 or 3 tablespoons of cheese cream. • Grill for a few minutes until the cheese has melted a little and the slices are slightly toasted.

Tapa de brie

Brie cheese

- 500 g Brie cheese
- 1 *chapata* (rustic-style bread)
- 6 teaspoons of olive oil, maximum acidity 0.4°
- 6 sprigs of rosemary

let's get started

Cut the bread diagonally to obtain longer slices and match the shape of the cheese. • Pour a few drops of oil onto each slice and cover with 6 triangles of Brie cheese. • Bake in the oven at 200° for 3 or 4 minutes.

Presentation: Garnish with a small sprig of rosemary.

Tapa de fritos de queso

Fried cheese

- Béchamel sauce (p. 114) made with 50 g flour
- 100g Gruyère cheese, grated
- 2 eggs, with the yolks separated from the egg white
- 4 pieces of sliced bread
- Abundant oil

let's get started

Remove the crust from the bread and cut each slice into 4 squares. • Prepare the béchamel sauce using 50 g flour and the other ingredients in the amounts indicated in the recipe. • Once prepared, leave until lukewarm and then add the beaten egg yolk and the grated cheese, stirring well. • Beat the egg white until stiff and slowly add to the béchamel sauce. • Spread the surface of the bread with the cream, making a little heap. Fry in abundant oil and eat immediately.

Tapa de queso y nueces
Cheese and walnuts

- 6 slices of bread
- 100g Roquefort cheese
- 50g Philadelphia-type cheese
- 100g butter, soft

- 100g walnuts
- 2 tablespoons cream
- Sprigs of tarragon

let's get started

Cheese cream: Soften the cheeses so that they can be blended with the butter and cream. • Set aside 12 walnuts for the garnish and grind the remaining ones in an electric blender. Add to the cheese mixture. Leave to cool in the refrigerator.

Presentation: Distribute the cheese cream on 6 pieces of bread and garnish with the whole walnuts and tarragon.

Tartaletas de aceitunas negras y sardinas
Black olive and sardine tartlets

- **12 pastry tartlets, readymade or home-made (see recipe, p. 118)**
- **150g black olives**

- **2 hard-boiled eggs**
- **85g sardines in olive oil, tinned**
- **2 tablespoons olive oil**

let's get started

Remove the stones from the olives and chop up as finely as possible. • Remove the scales and the central bone from the sardines. Chop up the sardines. • Boil the eggs for 12 minutes in salted water and shell under cold running water. Discard the yolks and chop up the whites. • Mix the olives, sardines and 1 or 2 tablespoons of oil, stirring well to achieve a consistent paste. This can be done in an electric blender.

Presentation: Fill the 12 tartlets with the olive and sardine mixture and garnish with a pile of chopped egg whites.

Volován caliente de torta del Casar
Hot ewe's milk cheese vol-au-vent

CHOOSE ONE OF THE FOLLOWING FOR THE FILLING:
• 6 cocktail vol-au-vents, 6 tartlets or 6 slices of bread

• 1 *torta del Casar* cheese (ewe's milk cheese)

let's get started

Choose your preferred base for the cheese. If you decide to make tartlets, consult the pastry recipe (p. 118). • Cocktail vol-au-vents are available in specialized stores. Heat for a few minutes in an oven. • Fill the tartlets or vol-au-vents to the brim with the cheese. • If you use bread, place the cheese on top. Finally, bake in the oven at 160°, removing as soon as the cheese begins to melt. This will take approximately 2 minutes.

Sauces, pastries and batters

Salsa alioli
Garlic and oil sauce

- **2 eggs**
- **1/4 l olive oil, maximum acidity 0.4°**
- **2 tablespoons water**
- **1 tablespoon red wine vinegar**

- **2 garlic cloves, chopped**
- **Salt**
- **A pinch of sugar**

let's get started

Beat the eggs in an electric blender or with a hand-held electric whisk. Remove the interior shoots from the garlic then chop up. Add the drops of oil, one by one at first, then add the garlic and continue to blend. As the mixture thickens, pour in small amounts of oil and continue blending until there is no oil left to add. Next, thin the sauce by adding the vinegar and water. Season and blend for a few more minutes to obtain an even consistency.

Salsa besamel
Béchamel sauce

- **40 cl olive oil, maximum acidity 0.4° or 50 g butter**
- **30 g flour**

- **1/2 l milk**
- **Salt**
- **Nutmeg**

let's get started

Boil the milk. • Pour the oil into a non-stick saucepan and lightly fry the flour. Add the milk in several portions, beating the mixture with a whisk and waiting until the mixture boils before adding more milk. • Once the mixture acquires a creamy consistency, season with grated nutmeg and salt.

Salsa de ahumados
Sauce for smoked dishes

- 2 dl mayonnaise sauce (see recipe, p. 116)
- 1 hard-boiled egg, chopped
- 1 tablespoon mild mustard (e.g. Savora)
- 2 tablespoons creamy yoghurt
- 1 tablespoon sugar
- 1 tablespoon dill, chopped
- Salt
- Pepper

let's get started

Prepare the mayonnaise. Add the creamy yoghurt, mustard, salt, sugar and ground pepper. Stir continuously to obtain an evenly-blended cream. Add the chopped hard-boiled egg and dill.

Salsa de tomate española
Spanish tomato sauce

- 2 dl olive oil
- 3 onions, chopped (approx. 250 g)
- 1 garlic clove, chopped
- 1 kg ripe tomatoes, sliced
- 1 laurel leaf (optional)
- Salt
- Sugar

let's get started

Lightly fry the onion in the oil and season with the salt and sugar. When transparent, add the garlic, tomatoes and laurel. • As they are cooking, mash the tomatoes with a skimmer. This sauce must simmer for 2 hours. When cooked, put through a sieve or food mill.
Note: Do not grind in an electric blender.

Salsa mayonesa

Mayonnaise sauce

- 2 whole eggs
- 1/2 l olive oil, maximum acidity 0.4°
- 1 teaspoon sherry vinegar
- 2 tablespoons water

- Salt
- Pepper
- A pinch of sugar

UTENSILS: **Electric blender**

let's get started

Place the eggs in the electric blender and add the oil drop by drop, blending continuously. As it thickens, pour in small amounts of oil and continue to blend until there is no oil left to add. Then add the water and vinegar and season. Blend for a few more minutes to obtain an even consistency.

Note: Wash the eggs thoroughly before use. During cool periods the sauce can be refrigerated for one week in a covered glass container.

Salsa rosa

Cocktail sauce

- 1/4 l mayonnaise sauce (see recipe, p. 116)
- 2 tablespoons tomato Ketchup

- 1 tablespoon brandy
- 1 Teaspoon sugar
- Salt

let's get started

Combine the mayonnaise with the remaining ingredients and beat for a few minutes.

Note: This sauce can be made with homemade or readymade mayonnaise. If you use the readymade variety, add the ingredients listed above plus two tablespoons of cream.

Crema para las crêpes
Pancake batter

- 125 g flour (12-14 pancakes)
- 2 eggs
- 1/4 l full milk
- Olive oil for frying

- Salt

UTENSILS:
Small 7 cm diameter frying pan and an electric blender

let's get started

Place all the ingredients in the electric blender. Mix well then leave to stand for 1 hour in the refrigerator. • Soak a piece of cotton wool in the oil to grease the frying pan then heat. When it is very hot, remove from the heat and pour in a tablespoon of batter, spreading it evenly around the pan. Return to the heat to allow the batter to set. Flip and cook on the other side. Repeat this process until all the pancake batter has been used.

Note: The pancakes can be made several days in advance and frozen in a pile, placing a sheet of tinfoil between each one.

Masa de buñuelos o pasta "choux"
Batter for fritters or choux pastry

- 1/4 l water
- 75 g butter

- 125 g flour
- 4 eggs
- Salt

let's get started

Boil the water with the butter and salt. When it starts to boil fiercely, quickly add all the flour. Lower the heat and stir continuously. The mixture should begin to separate from the sides of the pan and form a ball. The drier the mixture, the more the fritters or puffs will rise. Leave to cool a little then add the eggs one by one, waiting until the first egg is fully blended with the pastry before adding the next one, and so on until you have added all the eggs. • Heat the oven to 180° for 15 minutes. Grease the oven tray and lay out the pastry in small individual balls so that they do not stick together when they rise. Bake for 20 minutes. Remove a puff from the oven to check that it is sufficiently dry inside (the puffs will collapse if removed from the oven whilst still moist); if it is still moist, leave to bake for a little longer. • Once the puffs have cooled, they can be stored in a covered container.

Masa para empanadillas

Pastry for pasties

- 3 level tablespoons olive oil
- 3 level tablespoons milk
- 3 level tablespoons red wine

- 95 g (approx.) flour
- Salt

let's get started

Mix the liquid ingredients and season generously. • Add the flour, kneading manually to obtain a soft pastry. Leave to stand for 1 hour. • Sprinkle the table with flour and roll out the pastry very thinly with a rolling pin. Cut out circles measuring approximately 7 centimetres in diameter. • When you are ready to use them, stuff with a filling and fry in abundant oil.
Note: Readymade pasties are very convenient. This is also true of puff-pastry, which can be rolled out very thinly.

Masa quebrada

Pastry

- 250 g flour
- 125 g butter
- 1 egg yolk

- 3 tablespoons water
- Salt
- UTENSILS: **Individual baking moulds**

let's get started

Pour the flour into a large bowl and make a large hollow at the centre. Add to this hollow the butter (which should have a soft, creamy consistency), egg yolk, warm water and salt. Knead these ingredients manually, slowly folding in the flour to obtain a pastry. At this stage handle as little as possible. Leave to stand for 1 to 12 hours. Then sprinkle the table with flour and roll out the pastry with a rolling pin, beginning at the centre and rolling outwards to form a circle. Grease the moulds and line with pastry. To ensure that the pastry does not rise in the oven, pierce it with a fork and add a small ball wrapped in tinfoil. Leave to stand again in the refrigerator for approximately 10 minutes. • Bake in the oven for 15 to 25 minutes at 180°. Check regularly and when slightly golden, remove from the oven. • **Note:** It is possible to save time by buying frozen readymade pastry; however, the result will not be the same since homemade pastries, made with natural fats, always taste much better.

Subject index

93   Miscellaneous

113   Sauces, pastries and batters

Alphabetical index

Coordination and Production: ALDEASA
Text: Esperanza Luca de Tena
Translation: Polisemia
Photographs: © Cristina Rivarola
Estylism: Roser Domingo
          Cuca Roses
Series Design: Atela diseño gráfico
Layout: Aldeasa
Photomechanical Production: Lucam / Cromotex
Printed by: Brizzolis, arte en gráficas
© ALDEASA, 2010
I.S.B.N.: 978-84-8003-340-4
D.L.: M-23584-2010